Born to be Wild
Little Horses

Colette Barbé-Julien

Words that appear in the glossary are printed in
boldface type the first time they occur in the text.

GARETH**STEVENS**
PUBLISHING
A Member of the WRC Media Family of Companies

Off to a Good Start

A baby horse, which is called a foal, is already very athletic right after it is born. Although it is unsteady at first, a foal can stand on its long legs when it is only one hour old. Then the foal takes its first steps, moving closer to its mother so it can drink her milk. A foal also has very sharp senses. Thirty minutes after birth, it can move its ears around and hear noises, and unlike other animals whose eyes are closed at birth, a newborn foal can see its surroundings. Two hours after birth, a foal can "talk" to its mother by **neighing** and can understand when she neighs in return.

Before it is able to stand firmly on its long legs, a foal stands up and falls down several times. Its mother helps her baby stand by pushing it with her nose.

What do you think?

How old is a foal when it is able to run, or **gallop**?

a) four to five hours old

b) four to five days old

c) four to five months old

A foal is able to gallop when it is four to five hours old.

Foals are often born late at night, and by morning, they are able to run. Foals grow up fast. When they are six or seven months old, they already weigh half of what they will weigh as adults. The young horses then grow at a slower rate until they become adults. Horses are adults when they are three to five years old, depending on their **breed**. A male horse that is less than four years old is called a colt. A young female is called a filly. When female horses become adults, they are called mares.

A mare will carry a baby inside her body for about eleven months. In the ninth month, the future foal weighs about half of what it will weigh when it is born.

After a foal is born, the mare licks her baby to clean it. She sniffs the foal, then blows into its nostrils so the foal will learn her scent, too. The mare and the foal use the sense of smell to recognize each other.

4

When a foal is tired, it stretches out on the ground and falls asleep. Because its mother is always guarding the foal, she takes only light naps and remains standing.

A foal can do tricks! It can, for example, use one leg to scratch its ear, using the other three legs to keep its balance.

5

Living Together

Little horses spend lots of time playing. They run, jump, kick, and nibble at their friends and at their mothers. By playing together, foals learn how to communicate with other horses and how to live together in the same space. They must learn good manners and must not disturb mares that are **grazing** in the meadow. Foals must also learn that when horses live in a group, or **herd**, some horses are leaders, and the others must follow them and show them respect.

What do you think?

How does a foal show respect to the leader of its herd?

a) It bows slightly.

b) It moves its mouth as if it were chewing.

c) It backs up.

Mares on a farm or a horse ranch often live together in a meadow with their foals. The male horses that are the fathers of the foals live alone in other meadows or in **stables**. The male horses are called stallions.

Horses communicate with their bodies. By moving its nostrils, jaws, head, neck, legs, tail, or even its entire body, a horse can express fear, friendship, anger, obedience, or its wish to be the most powerful horse in its herd. When a horse points its ears forward, that means it is paying attention. Pointing its ears backward means the horse is scared. Foals quickly learn to understand signs like these and to obey the rules of the herd.

When they play, foals show their personalities and test their abilities. They learn which one of them is the strongest and which one is the fastest.

These foals are old enough to be separated from their mothers.
They grow stronger by racing with each other through the meadow.

An angry adult horse
can be dangerous.
Foals learn quickly
how to recognize this
danger and stay away.

As Hungry as a Horse

During the first days of its life, a foal will sometimes mistake another mare for its mother when it is hungry. Fortunately, its mother does not lose sight of the foal, and she will call to it to come eat. The mare's milk is a rich food but easy for the foal to **digest**, and it helps the foal grow up fast. In the wild, a foal drinks its mother's milk for about one year. It stops when the mare gives birth to another foal. On a farm or a ranch, the owner separates a foal from its mother when the foal is about six months old. The foal then begins to eat other foods.

A foal has to drink often because its mother's body can hold only a small amount of milk.

What do you think ?

When foals stop drinking their mother's milk, what do they eat?

a) grass and other plants

b) meat

c) yogurt and cheese

When they stop drinking their mothers' milk, foals eat grass and other plants.

In the wild, foals eat grass after they stop drinking their mother's milk. On farms and ranches, they eat grass and many other kinds of foods, including hay (which is grass that is cut and dried), cereals (such as barley and oats), and special kinds of dry foods that help horses grow and stay healthy. To encourage or reward a horse, its owner may give it treats such as carrots, apples, or bread. A horse can become very sick, however, if it eats too much.

A horse's strong sense of smell helps it find grass buried underneath snow. The horse will use its hoof to push the snow off the grass so it can eat.

Horses need to drink 10 to 12 gallons (38 to 45 liters) of clean, fresh water every day.

A foal learns from its mother how to avoid eating the types of grasses that are not good for its health.

Time to Be Trained

A herd of wild horses is led by either a stallion or an older mare. Horses on farms and ranches, however, are tamed and learn to follow humans as their leaders. At first, young foals are afraid of people and their surroundings, including noisy dogs, tractors, and cars, but little by little, the foals become used to these things. When they see their mothers being led by their owners, the foals quickly become used to being handled by people, too. A colt or a filly learns to trust its owner and to like having its owner groom, or brush, its coat every day. A foal also likes the treats its owner feeds it and will try to please its owner by following his or her commands.

What do you think?

Why does a horse sometimes nibble the arm of the person who is grooming it?

a) because the horse is pushy

b) because the horse is bored

c) because horses nibble when they groom each other

When a stall is left open, a foal will naturally want to run out the door. The foal's mother, however, teaches her baby to stay quietly by her side.

Horses nibble when they groom each other's coats.

Horses sometimes use their teeth to groom each other's coats, but they must learn not to nibble on the people who groom them — not even just to be friendly. The trust that develops between a foal and the person who grooms it is helpful when the foal's training begins. A horse starts being trained when it is only a few weeks old. First, it must learn to wear a halter and a lead. A halter is a set of leather straps that is worn on the horse's head. A lead is attached to the halter like a dog's leash is attached to a collar. When the horse is about one year old, it must wear a strap around its belly so it will begin to get used to the feeling of wearing a saddle. One or two years later, the horse will learn to be comfortable with a saddle on its back and reins and other equipment on its body.

When training a foal, the owner holds onto its lead.

The very first lesson a foal learns is to be guided by the person holding its lead. The foal is trained to walk forward and backward, to stop, and to turn. Later, the foal will learn to follow the same commands with a saddle and a rider on its back.

A foal is less frightened when it can explore the world with its mother. When the foal's mother is carrying a rider, the foal will often walk alongside her. This way, the foal learns to walk at the speed people like, instead of always running as fast as it can.

17

A Useful Life

When wild colts are two years old, they are pushed out of the herd by their father — the stallion that leads the herd. The colts will live with other young males until they attract females and start their own families. A wild herd's fillies start to **mate** when they are about two years old. The owners of tamed horses wait until their fillies are three or four years old before letting them mate. Both fillies and colts must first show their owners how fast and strong they are and how well they are able to run, jump, or pull carts or wagons. The best horses are picked for **breeding**. Horse owners want to make sure that each kind of horse passes on its special features and qualities to future foals. Purebred foals are those whose parents, and other family members before them, have all been the same breed.

A purebred foal is the most valuable and skilled. It begins racing or doing other work when it is only two years old. A purebred is at its peak between three and five years of age, when other colts and fillies are still being trained.

What do you think?

What is the difference in size between a colt and a filly?

a) Colts are taller than fillies.

b) Fillies are taller than colts.

c) There is no difference in size between a colt and a filly.

There is no difference in size between a colt and a filly.

The size of any horse depends on its breed. A full-grown Argentine Falabella is only about 30 inches (75 centimeters) tall, but this breed is still considered a horse, not a pony. The English Shire horse is a breed that grows to almost 6 feet (180 cm) tall and weighs more than a ton. People use horses based on the specialties of their breeds. Depending on whether a young horse is strong or **agile** or quiet or nervous, it will learn to carry riders, pull wagons, race, jump obstacles, perform in a circus, or herd cattle on a ranch.

Camargue horses are born with dark coats. When they are one year old, white hair begins to grow on their heads. At two years old, they are all gray. By the time they are adults, their coats are completely white.

Arabians are one of the oldest and most beautiful horse breeds. People living in the deserts of northern Africa and the Middle East have been raising Arabian horses for more than one thousand years. Arabian stallions are often bred with non-Arabian mares to improve other breeds.

The Percheron (*below*) is a draft horse. A long time ago, draft horses pulled plows in farm fields. Today, they pull carts and carriages. The Percheron is a smart and gentle breed and can be found everywhere in the world.

This beautiful horse from Andalusia, Spain, was trained for years before it could perform this trick.

Horses are **mammals.** More than 150 breeds of horses and ponies are found throughout the world. The different breeds of horses came about through gradual changes over a period of ten thousand years. The changes were due mainly to the climates where the horses lived. Hot areas produced tall, elegant horses, while cold areas produced short, strong ones. In dry areas, where grass is hard to find, horses are sleek and agile. In wet areas, where there is lots of grass to eat, horses are usually large and heavy. Most horses live twenty to twenty-five years.

Horses are related to donkeys, ponies, and zebras.

Horses have long, thick eyelashes that protect their eyes from dust and insects.

Horses use their long, strong tails to swat away insects.

The large joints on a horse's back legs are called hocks. The hocks are the joints that horses use the most.

Its mane gives a horse protection against bad weather and helps it swat away insects.

Horses move their ears to hear sounds coming from many different directions.

With their large nostrils, horses can breathe in a lot of air.

A horse has a strong sense of touch. It even uses the hair around its **muzzle** to feel.

The coat of a horse has overlapping hair that protects the animal from bad weather. A horse grows a thicker coat every fall, then sheds hair in spring.

The legs of a horse must be straight and strong to support the animal's weight and for the horse to run properly.

A horse's hoof is a single toe covered with a thick layer of material that is a lot like a human fingernail.

GLOSSARY

agile — able to move quickly and easily

breed — (n) a particular group of animals that all have the same physical features and abilities

breeding — (v) mating

digest — to break down food into a form that can be absorbed and used by the body

gallop — to run on four legs at a fast speed

grazing — feeding on growing grass and other plants

herd — a group of one kind of animal that stays together

mammals — warm-blooded animals that have backbones, give birth to live babies, feed their young with milk from the mother's body, and are usually covered with hair or fur

mate — (v) to join together to produce young

muzzle — the front of the head of some animals, such as horses and dogs, which sticks out and on which the animal's nose and mouth are located

neighing — making the high-pitched sound of a horse

reins — long leather straps attached to a piece of metal in a horse's mouth, which are held and moved by a rider or driver to control the horse

stables — buildings used to shelter animals such as horses

Please visit our web site at: www.garethstevens.com
For a free color catalog describing Gareth Stevens Publishing's list of high-quality books and multimedia programs, call 1-800-542-2595 (USA) or 1-800-387-3178 (Canada). Gareth Stevens Publishing's fax: (414) 332-3567.

Library of Congress Cataloging-in-Publication Data

Barbé-Julien, Colette.
  [Poulain. English]
  Little horses / Colette Barbé-Julien. — North American ed.
    p. cm. — (Born to be wild)
  ISBN 0-8368-6167-1 (lib. bdg.)
  1. Foals—Juvenile literature. 2. Horses—Juvenile literature.
  I. Title. II. Series.
  SF302.B3613 2006
  636.1'07—dc22   2005053154

This North American edition first published in 2006 by
Gareth Stevens Publishing
A Member of the WRC Media Family of Companies
330 West Olive Street, Suite 100
Milwaukee, Wisconsin 53212 USA

This U.S. edition copyright © 2006 by Gareth Stevens, Inc.
Original edition copyright © 2003 by Mango Jeunesse.

First published in 2003 as *Le poulain* by Mango Jeunesse, an imprint of Editions Mango, Paris, France. Additonal end matter copyright © 2006 by Gareth Stevens, Inc.

Picture Credits (t=top, b=bottom, l=left, r=right)
Bios: D. Halleux title page, 8, 9(t), back cover; Klein/Hubert 12(both). Cogis: Miriski 2, 4(l), 17(t); Labat 9(b); Beroule 10, 16; Varin 15; Hermeline 18; Farissier 21(br). Colibri: L. Gineste cover; A. Gioanni 5(t); C. Baranger 5(b); J. Berquez 13; J. Joannet 17(b); A. M. Loubsens 20, 21(t), 22-23; S. Bonneau 21(bl); F. & J. L. Ziegler 22. Sunset: G. Lacz 4(r); Horizon Vision 7.

English translation: Muriel Castille
Gareth Stevens editor: Barbara Kiely Miller
Gareth Stevens art direction: Tammy West
Gareth Stevens designer: Jenni Gaylord

Printed in the United States of America

1 2 3 4 5 6 7 8 9 10 09 08 07 06